Smithsonian

PLYMOUTH ROCK

What an Artifact Can Tell Us About the Story of the Pilgrims

by Nel Yomtov

Broken from the MOTHER ROCK by Mr LEWIS BRADFORD, on TUESDAY 28th of Decr 1830. 4¼ o clock P.M., SCADDING. the PILGRIMS MR SHAW. Whitney RICH. Landed upon thi ROCK Decr 11th I. 20. os

CAPSTONE PRESS
a capstone imprint

Capstone Captivate is published by Capstone Press,
an imprint of Capstone.
1710 Roe Crest Drive
North Mankato, Minnesota 56003
www.capstonepub.com

Library of Congress Cataloging-in-Publication Data
Names: Yomtov, Nelson, author.
Title: Plymouth Rock : what an artifact can tell us about the story of the pilgrims / by Nel Yomtov.
Description: North Mankato, Minnesota : Capstone Press, [2021] | Series: Artifacts from the American past | Includes bibliographical references and index. | Audience: Ages: 8-11 | Audience: Grades: 4-6 | Summary: "Plymouth Rock has long stood as a symbol of the Pilgrims' journey to and settlement in America. But how much of the story surrounding it is true? What did the Pilgrims' arrival mean to the Wampanoag people who were already living there? What were the long-lasting effects of the interactions between the two groups? How did a seaside rock come to be associated with the Pilgrims' landing, and was it really part of their story at all? Readers will find out the answers to these questions and discover more of what Plymouth Rock can tell us about American history"—Provided by publisher.
Identifiers: LCCN 2021002461 (print) | LCCN 2021002462 (ebook) | ISBN 9781496695413 (hardcover) | ISBN 9781496696830 (paperback) | ISBN 9781977154743 (pdf) | ISBN 9781977156402 (kindle edition)
Subjects: LCSH: Pilgrims (New Plymouth Colony)—Juvenile literature. | Wampanoag Indians—Massachusetts—Juvenile literature. | Plymouth Rock (Plymouth, Mass.)—Juvenile literature. | Massachusetts—History—New Plymouth, 1620-1691—Juvenile literature.
Classification: LCC F68 .Y678 2021 (print) | LCC F68 (ebook) | DDC 974.4/02—dc23
LC record available at https://lccn.loc.gov/2021002461
LC ebook record available at https://lccn.loc.gov/2021002462

Image Credits
Associated Press: Lisa Poole, 42; Bridgeman Images: 29, © Look and Learn, 9, Peter Newark American Pictures, 23; Getty Images: Archive Photos/Kean Collection/Harold M. Lambert, cover (back), The Boston Globe/John Tlumacki, 39; iStockphoto: duncan1890, 24, 30, ivan-96, 20, TonyBaggett, 12, traveler1116, 5, whitemay, 13; Library of Congress: 15, 16, 19, 21, 32, 36; The New York Public Library: 22, 41; Newscom: Danita Delimont Photography/Angel Wynn, 7, 35; North Wind Picture Archives, 8, 10, 17, 26; Shutterstock: Marcio Jose Bastos Silva, 43, Michael Sean OLeary, 31, 44, nobeastsofierce, 11, PhotoItaliaStudio, 45; Smithsonian Institution: National Museum of American History, 38, National Museum of American History/Virginia L. W. Fox, cover (bottom right), 1, 37, National Portrait Gallery, 33; XNR Productions: 14

Editorial Credits
Editor: Mandy Robbins; Designer: Tracy Davies; Media Researcher: Svetlana Zhurkin; Production Specialist: Tori Abraham

Smithsonian Credits
Barbara Clark Smith, Museum Curator, Division of Political, National Museum of American History; Bethanee Bemis, Museum Specialist, Division of Political History, National Museum of American History

All internet sites appearing in back matter were available and accurate when this book was sent to press.

TABLE OF CONTENTS

Words in **bold** are in the glossary.

Chapter 1
AN ENDURING MYTH

For many years, U.S. students were taught that in 1620, Pilgrims sailed from England to North America. They landed in what is now Massachusetts. The passengers aboard the *Mayflower* had made the dangerous journey across the Atlantic Ocean. They were looking for a place to practice their religion freely. As the ship approached land, the Pilgrims nervously eyed the New World for the first time. According to the story, the newcomers stepped ashore and set foot on an enormous rock—Plymouth Rock.

This story of the Pilgrims and Plymouth Rock has been around for hundreds of years. The rock itself has become a symbol of the United States, like the Statue of Liberty and the Liberty Bell. But is the story true? Apparently not. In fact, no historical evidence shows that the Pilgrims landed on Plymouth Rock. It turns out that for many years, U.S. schoolchildren were taught a myth.

So what is the truth behind the myth? What can Plymouth Rock tell us about the Pilgrims and the New World?

An 1896 engraving shows the *Mayflower* approaching Plymouth Rock.

Chapter 2
THE WAMPANOAG EXPERIENCE

The myth of Plymouth Rock painted the New World as an empty wilderness. But the truth was that the area was already home to an established American Indian society called the Wampanoag Nation. Wampanoags had lived in present-day Rhode Island and Massachusetts for thousands of years. They also made their home on several nearby islands. When the Pilgrims arrived, there were about 2,000 Wampanoags on the mainland and 3,000 on nearby islands.

By the time the English arrived in the early 1600s, the Wampanoags had an established **civilization**. For hundreds of years, they had hunted, fished, farmed, and traded with other Native peoples. They had organized villages, roadways, and storage pits for crops. They grew corn, beans, and squash on well-tended planting fields. The area was their home.

Wampanoags traditionally ate berries and clams that they gathered.

Wampanoags had contact with Europeans long before the Pilgrims arrived in 1620. Explorers from Europe made contact with them starting in the early 1520s. Over time, more and more white men came to the area. Meetings with European explorers and traders happened frequently in the early 1600s. These meetings didn't always go well.

A European explorer approaches a New England harbor in the 1500s.

The reason for the meetings was trade. Europeans wanted animal furs and fresh food. Wampanoags traded these items for the Europeans' glass beads and metal jewelry, such as rings and bracelets. The trades, however, often ended in violence. Because of the great cultural differences, the Wampanoags and the Europeans did not trust each other. The meetings often ended in murder, kidnapping, and enslavement on both sides.

European explorers traded with American Indians.

Contact with the Europeans brought an even deadlier problem for American Indians—disease. For hundreds of years, people in Europe had faced deadly diseases, such as **smallpox**, plague, and **typhus**. Over time, many Europeans developed **resistance** to these diseases. Even with resistance, these diseases can kill people. The American Indians had never faced these horrible illnesses before. They had no resistance to them at all.

Great numbers of Wampanoags suffered and died from European diseases.

The **epidemic** of 1616 to 1619 destroyed many Wampanoag communities. As many as 90 percent of the Wampanoag people died during this time. Entire villages were wiped out. Farmlands lay in ruins. The disease wiped out so many Wampanoag people that they were no longer able to defend their lands against other American Indian Nations. By the time the Pilgrims arrived, the Wampanoags were in a weakened state.

What Disease Caused the Epidemic of the Early 1600s?

Many scientists believe smallpox was responsible for the epidemic of the early 1600s. Smallpox causes fever, headaches, and painful sores. The sores appear all over the body, as well as in the throat and mouth. Smallpox spreads when a person coughs, sneezes, or speaks. It can also spread when someone touches the clothing or bedsheets of a sick person.

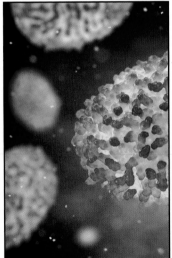

Smallpox is caused by the Variola virus.

Chapter 3
A HISTORIC LANDING

At the same time, in England, another group of people faced a difficult situation. They were called Separatists. They believed the Church of England was **corrupt**. Many broke from the Church and moved to Holland in 1608. They worshipped freely there. But they wanted to find a more remote place to live. They thought their children were becoming too much like the Dutch people around them. They didn't like it. They wanted to have more control over how they lived.

The Pilgrims left Delft Haven, Holland, on the *Mayflower* voyage in 1620.

On September 6, 1620, the Separatists boarded a ship called the *Mayflower*. It was headed for America. Of the 102 people on board, about 40 were Separatists. Today we call them Pilgrims. They wanted freedom to practice their own religion, separate from the Church of England. They wanted a place where their church would be in control. The other passengers wanted freedom, adventure, and a fresh start in the New World.

A secret meeting of the Separatists in England

Separatists and Religious Freedom

The Separatists set up their own churches in England. They believed that a church should be established by God's will, not by the state, like the Church of England had been. Each Separatist church ran its own affairs. The Separatist movement was illegal in England in the early 1600s. Followers were often mistreated by the state and the Church of England.

The *Mayflower*'s trip across the Atlantic Ocean took nine weeks. The travelers had planned to land in present-day New York State. At the time, the location was part of the English colony of Virginia. But on November 9, 1620, the ship came upon Cape Cod in Massachusetts. The sailors tried to head south to their landing stop at the Hudson River. But rough seas forced them to stay and explore Cape Cod.

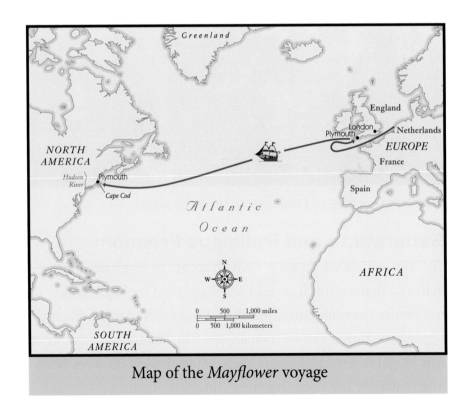

Map of the *Mayflower* voyage

The *Mayflower* dropped anchor and spent the next month or so offshore. Scouting parties went ashore to find wood and water. They discovered signs of American Indians living there, including Wampanoag graves. They took things from abandoned Native homes and stole food from underground storage pits.

The travelers tried landing at other spots, but none seemed right for starting a colony. Finally, they found what is now Plymouth Harbor. It was just right.

The Mayflower in Plymouth Harbor by William Formby Halsall

FACT!
Pilgrim scouting parties often dug into Wampanoag graves. They stole items left with the bodies. One Pilgrim's journal reported taking "the prettiest things away with us," which included bracelets, bowls, and trinkets.

In December of 1620, the *Mayflower* entered Plymouth Harbor. The landing spot was a flat, sandy beach. The only noticeable rock was a huge boulder at the base of a hill.

The area had a brook and **deserted** planting fields. The Pilgrims didn't know the fields were empty because the epidemic had killed the earlier residents. They built their settlement on land that was once a Wampanoag cornfield. The Pilgrims thought the land was abandoned and decided it was theirs for the taking. They built mud and wood shelters.

The Pilgrims came ashore during a cold New England winter.

Most of the passengers lived on the ship for the next few months. They moved back and forth between the *Mayflower* and the land as they built the settlement of Plymouth. The men hunted and fished for food. No one could imagine the days of hunger and hardship that they would face at Plymouth Colony.

The Pilgrims struggled to survive during their first year in the New World.

Chapter 4
THE PILGRIM EXPERIENCE

Many of the English colonists had fallen ill during the trip. Others got sick shortly after arriving at Plymouth. Some suffered **scurvy**. This disease is caused by a lack of vitamin C, which is found in fruits and vegetables. Others caught **pneumonia** during the cold, wet New England winter. Two or three people died each day during their first few weeks at Plymouth. Fewer than half of the passengers would survive the first year in the New World.

Without help, all of the settlers could die of illness and hunger. The Wampanoags were their only hope. Based on their earlier meetings with Europeans, the Wampanoags were afraid of the colonists. They wanted to trade with the newcomers, but they kept their distance during the early days of the colony. The Wampanoags could easily have overrun the settlers, in their weakened state.

Pilgrims walking through a snowy landscape to the church

Plymouth Colony Growth

December 1620: 102 colonists arrive at Plymouth Harbor and start the Plymouth Colony.

Winter 1620-1621: More than half of the colonists die of illness.

November 1621: A ship arrives with 35 new colonists.

July 1623: Another 90 colonists arrive in Plymouth.

1629-1630: Numerous ships bring about 1,000 new colonists. Many returned to England or moved to other newly established colonies.

1630: The total population of Plymouth Colony is about 300.

1633: The total population of Plymouth Colony reaches 400.

The first direct contact between the English and the Wampanoags came in March 1621. Massosoit, the Wampanoag leader, made a visit to the colony. His full name was Ousamequin. After exchanging gifts and sharing a meal, the two parties signed a **treaty**. According to the treaty, neither party was to harm the other. If any goods had been stolen, they would be returned. The two parties would also be **allies** in times of war.

Massosoit interacts with Pilgrim leaders.

As a show of good faith, a Wampanoag man named Tisquantum went to live with the colonists. Today he is known as Squanto. He had been kidnapped by English sailors years earlier. Squanto had spent several years in England and had learned English. Squanto taught the Pilgrims how to farm, hunt, and fish effectively. This knowledge helped them survive their first year in Plymouth. In November 1621, 35 new colonists arrived. Plymouth had hopes for a brighter future.

A 1914 depiction of the Pilgrims' Thanksgiving feast with the Wampanoags

The First Thanksgiving

In late September or early October of 1621, the colonists enjoyed a large harvest feast. There were heaps of food and military drills. Some sources say that upon hearing gunshots, a group of armed Wampanoag men rushed to the colony, fearing it was under attack. When they saw that it was not, the Wampanoags joined the celebration. For the next several days, the two groups celebrated and ate together as friends.

The Pilgrims were very religious. They believed that they had been chosen by God to lead Christians around the world. Though they had signed a treaty, they thought they were better than the Wampanoags. Because of this, they started to take advantage of their relationship with them. The Pilgrims believed they had a God-given right to take the Wampanoag's land. At first, this land was just the cleared fields left empty by the Wampanoags' recent sickness.

Plymouth Colony in 1622

Pilgrim settlers made unfair deals with the Wampanoags.

The Pilgrims' attitude made the relationship with the Wampanoags a tense one. The Pilgrims traded coats, knives, shoes, and axes for other large pieces of land. These were unfair trades. The Wampanoags thought the Pilgrims wanted access to the land, not to control it completely. As the English moved farther into Wampanoag lands, tensions flared. The two groups often fought. But the Pilgrims continued taking Wampanoag land.

For many years, the Wampanoags tried to set limits to Pilgrims' expanding settlement. But eventually, the colonizers overran the Wampanoags and other New England tribes. They pushed the remaining American Indian Nations out of the area.

Over time, the Pilgrims overcame many hardships—brutal winters, starvation, and deadly illnesses—and they built a successful colony. Plymouth grew as new colonists arrived. The Pilgrims had shown that they could thrive in a harsh new environment. Inspired by their success, more Europeans came to the New World. Larger colonies and towns sprung up in the area.

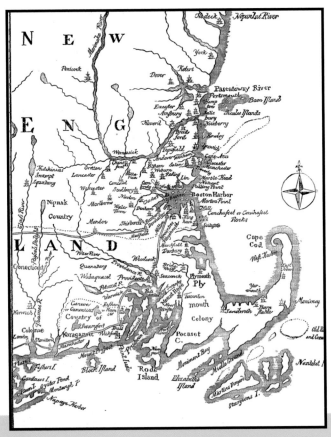

A map of New England in the 1700s marked with European settlements

Later generations of Americans claimed the Pilgrims brought the idea of freedom to the New World. They began to see the Pilgrims as lovers of liberty. Roger Wolcott, the governor of Connecticut during the 1750s, said, "Their feeble plantation became the birthplace of religious liberty, the cradle of a free Commonwealth. To them a mighty nation owes its debt." The Pilgrims came to symbolize endurance and strength—like Plymouth Rock itself.

The Pilgrim's New World experience was a success. But its cost to American Indian lives and societies was swept aside and forgotten by colonists. The myth of Plymouth Rock focused only on the Pilgrims' historic landing. It ignored the violence and theft of American Indian lands. It was just the beginning of the white mans' destruction of the Native Americans' ways of life.

FACT!

In 1920 and 1921, the U.S. government issued a 50-cent coin called the Pilgrim half-dollar. The coin marked the 300th anniversary of the arrival of the Pilgrims in the New World.

Chapter 5
THE LEGEND OF PLYMOUTH ROCK

Legend has it that the Pilgrims landed near a giant rock at Plymouth Harbor. They were said to have stepped upon it as they came off the *Mayflower*. But there is a problem with this story.

The Pilgrims coming ashore at Plymouth Rock

There were only two firsthand accounts written about the Pilgrims' landing. Neither one mentions that anyone came ashore on a rock. So where did this long-lasting tale come from, and how did it become accepted as fact?

The legend of Plymouth Rock was born in 1769. A man named Ephraim Spooner told a gathering of Plymouth citizens about something that he had seen as a boy. According to Spooner, the town of Plymouth was planning to build a wharf on the waterfront in 1741. The wharf would have buried a large rock. When 95-year-old resident Thomas Fraunce heard the news about the new wharf, he told the townspeople, including young Ephraim, a surprising story.

> **FACT!**
> The most detailed account of the Pilgrims' landing is William Bradford's journal, *Of Plimouth Plantation*. It was written between 1630 and 1650. Bradford was the second governor of Plymouth Colony.

Fraunce said the large rock was the same one that his father had claimed the Pilgrims stepped upon as they landed at Plymouth. He begged the townspeople to save the rock. But they built the wharf anyway. A small hump of the rock remained above ground. The rock remained ignored at the time. Fraunce's tale about Plymouth Rock, however, spread quickly.

It wasn't until the early 1770s that Plymouth Rock became popular. The spirit of the American Revolution was sweeping across New England. The leaders in Plymouth decided to move the rock to the Liberty Pole in the town square. Liberty Poles were symbols of the Americans' fight for freedom from Great Britain. The huge granite stone, however, split in two as it was being moved. The bottom part was left at the wharf. The top was brought into town. Patriotic Americans saw the split as a symbol of the separation between England and the colonies. Plymouth Rock was becoming an important national symbol.

> ### FACT!
> Weight estimates of the original, full-sized Plymouth Rock in 1620 range from 40 to 200 tons.

During the American Revolution (1775–1783), patriots
viewed Plymouth Rock as a symbol of independence.

In 1834, the rock broke again during a move to Pilgrim Hall Museum. Souvenir hunters chipped off pieces. In 1859, construction began on a **canopy** to house the part of the rock at the wharf. When the bottom piece was about to be placed inside the canopy, it was too large to fit. The rock was cut down further. One huge piece ended up as a doorstep at a local historic house. In 1880, the upper part was hauled from town and set on top of the piece in the canopy. The date "1620" was carved into the top part.

An engraving of the monument with the stone canopy marking the Pilgrims' landing in Plymouth, Massachusetts

Over the years, Plymouth Rock became one of the most important American symbols.

In 1920, the old wharf was removed and the waterfront was rebuilt. The rock was taken from its canopy. It was kept in a warehouse while a new monument was built at the water's edge. In 1921, Plymouth Rock was placed beneath the monument, where it sits today. The rock is partly buried in the sand. Twice a day it's covered in water as the tides come in. The rock now weighs about 10 tons.

Chapter 6
THE MAKING OF A LEGEND

The legend of Plymouth Rock spread across America. Popular plays of the early 1800s showed the Pilgrims carving the date of the landing on the rock. Several well-known paintings showed the Pilgrims standing on the rock as they came ashore. *Landing of the Pilgrim Fathers* (1850), painted by Charles Lucy, an English artist, is among the most famous.

Landing of the Pilgrim Fathers by Charles Lucy

In 1820, Daniel Webster, the nation's leading speaker, delivered a speech in Plymouth to celebrate the 200th anniversary of the landing.

"Beneath us is the rock, on which New England received the feet of the Pilgrims," said Webster. He also praised the Pilgrims for their "high religious faith" and "those principles of civil and religious liberty."

His speech was reported in many newspapers. It has had a lasting impact on the connection between the rock and the landing of the Pilgrims. We know now, however, that many of the events described in these plays, paintings, or speeches are not true.

The Words of a Famous Speaker

In 1824, statesman Edward Everett delivered a speech at Plymouth. Everett was the most famous speaker in the country at the time. He promoted the myth of Plymouth Rock by claiming the Pilgrims landed on "the ice-clad rocks of Plymouth." Copies of Everett's speech were distributed as far away as England.

Edward Everett

As Plymouth Rock continued to gain fame and importance, Wampanoags struggled to survive. Many who were not killed in early conflicts were captured and sold into slavery. Colonial courts forced Wampanoags out of the area for crimes such as theft and assault. Colonists accused of these crimes were often given only fines. Wampanoags who owed money were often forced to work for free until the bills were paid. Sometimes children were made servants to help pay their parents' bills. Many Wampanoags were forced to live on faraway **reservations**. Some Wampanoag communities disappeared entirely, as members were forced onto reservations or went to live amongst white people.

A few Wampanoag communities survived the horrors of war and colonization. Some worked for colonists. They provided a cheap source of labor. Today about 4,000 to 5,000 Wampanoag people live in New England. Roughly half, or 2,600, belong to the Mashpee Wampanoag Tribe. Some live on Mashpee reservation lands in Massachusetts.

A member of the Mashpee Wampanoag Tribe works with a horse at the Mashpee's Equestrian Center.

FACT!

The Mashpee Wampanoag Tribe traces its roots in the Massachusetts and Rhode Island area as far back as 12,000 years.

Chapter 7
A PERMANENT HOME

By 1911, two large pieces of Plymouth Rock had found a home at the Smithsonian Institution's National Museum of American History in Washington, D.C. The first piece measures 4 by 2 inches (10 by 5 centimeters). A relative of Governor William Bradford of Plymouth Colony chipped it from the original rock. This piece is painted with a label that reads, "Broken from the Mother Rock by Mr. Lewis Bradford on Tues. 28th of Dec. 1850 4 ½ o'clock p.m." Gustavus Vasa Fox, an officer of the U.S. Navy, owned the rock. The Fox family donated it to the Smithsonian in 1911. It is not known how Fox came to own the rock.

Gustavus Vasa Fox in 1866

The piece of Plymouth Rock donated by the Fox family

Souvenirs of Granite

Pieces of Plymouth Rock can be found throughout the United States and beyond. A 50-pound (22.7-kilogram) piece sits in a church in Brooklyn, New York. Some pieces were taken to Immingham, England. This is where the Pilgrims left for Holland. Another large piece was broken up and became part of a concrete floor. Paperweights, earrings, and cuff links have been made from Plymouth Rock too.

The second piece of Plymouth Rock in the Smithsonian's collection is much larger than the first. It measures 21.5 inches long (54.6 cm) and weighs 100 pounds (45.4 kg). In the 1920s, the Plymouth Antiquarian Society purchased the 1677 Harlow House on Sandwich Street in Plymouth. This group collects very old, rare objects. A 400-pound (181.4-kg) piece of the rock was found on their property. It was being used as a doorstop. The society chipped off a piece of the rock and carried it to Boston. An expert who had worked on souvenir pieces of the rock pronounced it to be a real piece of Plymouth Rock.

The other piece of the Plymouth Rock doorstop sits at the National Museum of American History.

A young visitor at Pilgrim Hall in Plymouth touches the famed Plymouth Rock.

In 1984, the society gave the Smithsonian the piece of the old doorstop. The remaining chunk, just less than 300 pounds (136 kg), is on display at Pilgrim Hall in Plymouth. Years earlier, pieces of this remaining rock at Harlow House were chipped off to make paperweights. The society sold the paperweights for $10 each to help pay for repairs to the building.

Chapter 8
THE SYMBOLIC ROCK OF PLYMOUTH

Plymouth Rock is more than a simple piece of stone. It has been used as a symbol for many causes and movements in United States history. In 1774, patriots viewed the accidental splitting of the rock as a symbol of the colonies' split from England.

In the 1800s, **abolitionists** used Pilgrims and Plymouth Rock as symbols in their fight against slavery. They held many antislavery meetings in Plymouth. They praised the freedom-seeking Pilgrim spirit and tradition. They urged people to recapture that spirit and work to end slavery.

When slavery was finally brought to an end in 1865, some people referred to Plymouth Rock in a symbolic way. In a 1893 speech, Frederic Taylor said, "It was with a rough and jagged piece of Plymouth Rock . . . that Abraham Lincoln shattered the **manacle** of the slave." The rejoining of the two halves of Plymouth Rock in 1880 represented the reunion of North and South after the Civil War (1861–1865).

The old canopy monument housed Plymouth Rock in the 1800s.

Plymouth Rock was a positive symbol to many, but it meant something very different to others. To many American Indians, the arrival of the Pilgrims did not symbolize the birth of freedom in the New World. The Pilgrims' landing was not "a day to celebrate but rather one to **mourn**," said William Apess, a New England Pequot Indian, in 1836. Today, many American Indians of New England observe the fourth Thursday of November—Thanksgiving Day—as the National Day of Mourning.

A crowd observes the National Day of Mourning in Plymouth, Massachusetts.

Plymouth Rock is one of America's oldest symbols. It represents an important event in the nation's history. For many Americans, the rock stands for courage and faith. For others, it represents the destruction of New England's American Indian nations. Perhaps it can best be seen as a reminder that historical myths and historical facts can often be confused.

Tourists visit Plymouth Rock in Plymouth, Massachusets.

FACT!

In 1970 and again in 1995, groups of American Indian protestors dumped sand on Plymouth Rock and buried it. "It was the start of everything bad that has happened to the American Indian," said an 18-year-old member of the Mohawk Nation in 1970.

EXPLORE MORE

A replica of a Wampanoag home at Plimouth Plantation

Plimouth Patuxet

Located on Plymouth's waterfront, Plimouth Patuxet is a living history museum that recreates the original Plymouth Colony of the 1600s. The museum features a Pilgrim village and several types of Wampanoag homes. The *Mayflower II*, a full-sized reproduction of the original *Mayflower*, is open to the public at Plymouth's waterfront. Patuxet is the Wampanoag name for the site of the Plymouth Colony.

Pilgrim Hall Museum

Pilgrim Hall Museum

The Pilgrim Hall Museum in Plymouth, Massachusetts, displays Pilgrim and American Indian artifacts. These include cookware, swords, guns, embroidery, medical instruments, and American Indian documents.

Sacrifice Rock

Sacrifice Rock is another important rock in Plymouth. Hundreds of years before the arrival of the Pilgrims, Wampanoag travelers left small branches or stones on top of the rock as a sacrifice, or to request the blessing of safe passage. The rock is located on Old Sandwich Road in Plymouth, Massachusetts.

GLOSSARY

abolitionist (ab-uh-LI-shuhn-ist)—a person who worked to end slavery

ally (AL-eye)—a country that supports another during a war

canopy (KAN-uh-pee)—an overhead roof that provides shelter

civilization (si-vuh-ly-ZAY-shuhn)—an organized and advanced society

corrupt (kuh-RUHPT)—dishonest behavior

deserted (di-ZUR-tid)—empty of people

epidemic (eh-puh-DEH-mik)—an infectious disease that spreads quickly through a community or population group

manacle (MAN-ih-kuhl)—a shackle for fastening someone's hands or ankles

mourn (MORN)—to be very sad and miss someone who has died or something that has been lost

pneumonia (noo-MOH-nyuh)—an infection of the lungs

reservation (rez-er-VAY-shuhn)—an area set aside as a homeland for American Indians and Alaska natives

resistance (rih-ZISS-tuhnss)—the attempt to overcome something

scurvy (SKUR-vee)—a deadly disease caused by lack of vitamin C

smallpox (SMAWL-poks)—a contagious viral disease that causes people's skin to break out in blisters and leaves deep scars

treaty (TREE-tee)—a formal agreement between groups

typhus (TY-fuhss)—a severe disease that causes fever, headache, weakness, coughing, and a dark red rash

READ MORE

Isbell, Hannah. *Squanto: Native American Translator and Guide.* Berkeley Heights, NJ: Enslow Publishing, 2018.

Lajiness, Katie. *Wampanoag.* Minneapolis, MN: Abdo Publishing, 2017.

Siegel, Rebecca. *Mayflower: The Ship That Started a Nation.* London: The Quarto Group, 2020.

Uhl, Xina M., and J. Poolos. *A Primary Source Investigation of the Mayflower.* New York: Rosen Central, 2019.

INTERNET SITES

The Mayflower and Plymouth Colony
ushistory.org/us/3a.asp

Plymouth Colony Facts for Kids
kids.kiddle.co/Plymouth_Colony

Who Were the Pilgrims?
plimoth.org/learn/just-kids/homework-help/who-were-pilgrims

INDEX